SHANGHAI
THE CITY AT A GLANCE

Suzhou Creek
This historic shipping route snakes throu
the city, starting at the Bund and passing
through the gallery district, Moganshan Lu.

Shimao International Plaza
Home to the 770-room Le Royal Méridien
hotel, this futuristic tower, opened in 2006,
anchors People's Park and Nanjing Lu.
819 Nanjing Donglu

Oriental Pearl TV Tower
Built in 1994 to launch the newly developed
Pudong district, Shanghai's 468m broadcast
antenna has become its defining landmark.
See p010

Urban Planning Exhibition Center
Head here to view the future: a large-scale
model of the city as it could look in 2020.
See p034

SWFC (Shanghai World Financial Center)
Currently the tallest building in China, the
SWFC in Pudong is instantly recognisable
thanks to its bottle-opener-like top.
See p013

Shanghai Museum
Hugely popular, this museum houses a fine
collection of Chinese artefacts and antiques,
and appropriately resembles a giant
cauldron with handles on all four sides.
201 Renmin Dadao

Concert Hall
Opened in 1930, this 1,200-seater concert hall
is part of the cluster of cultural buildings in
People's Park. It was lifted and moved 66.4m
in 2002 to make way for the adjacent highway.
523 Yan'an Donglu

INTRODUCTION
THE CHANGING FACE OF THE URBAN SCENE

Shanghai's story has always been one of extremes. As one of the spoils of British victory in the first Opium War, the city was dubbed the 'Whore of the Orient'. Severely chastened by the 'Liberation', it became an ultra-left base for Madame Mao during the Cultural Revolution. By the 1980s it was searching furiously for its modern self, constructing China's sleekest new structures while at the same time reimagining the most significant buildings of its past.

At various points in history, this city has been the biggest metropolis in the world, and today it's growing at a formidable rate. In 2008, the SWFC (see p013) pierced the Pudong skyline, and ground was broken for an even taller skyscraper, the 632m Shanghai Tower, designed by the American firm Gensler. Financed in cash by three local companies, the project was a sure sign that, in spite of the global crash, Shanghai surges on. The growing reputation of its creative community and its art and design fairs, such as SHContemporary (www.shcontemporary.info) and 100% Design Shanghai (www.100percentdesign.com.cn), also signals the city's naked ambition. Beijing may be where most of the artists live, but Shanghai is where the business is done.

The World Expo 2010, which the city hosted on the banks of the Huangpu, was a status-defining event. Unsurprisingly, China's pavilion was the tallest of the lot. The Expo confirmed that to visit Shanghai now is to see the epitome of Chinese globalisation.

ESSENTIAL INFO
FACTS, FIGURES AND USEFUL ADDRESSES

TOURIST OFFICE
Luwan District Service Center
127 Chengdu Lu
T 5386 1882
www.meet-in-shanghai.net

TRANSPORT
Metro
T 6437 0000
Trains run until 11.30pm daily
Taxis
Qiangsheng
T 6258 0000
Taxis can also be hailed on the street

EMERGENCY SERVICES
Ambulance
T 120
Fire
T 119
Police
T 110
Late-night pharmacy (until 9pm)
Hua Shi
1376 Nanjing Xilu
T 6279 8090

CONSULATES
British Consulate-General
Suite 301, Shanghai Center, 1376 Nanjing Xilu
T 6279 7650
www.uk.cn/bj
US Consulate
8th floor, 1038 Nanjing Xilu
T 3217 4650
shanghai.usembassy-china.org.cn

MONEY
American Express
Room 455, Shanghai Center, 1376 Nanjing Xilu
T 6279 7072
travel.americanexpress.com

POSTAL SERVICES
Post office
276 Beisuzhou Lu
T 6393 6666
Shipping
UPS
T 3896 5599
www.ups.com

BOOKS
New China, New Art by Richard Vine
(Prestel)
Shanghai by Alan Balfour and Zheng
Shiling (Wiley-Academy)
**Shanghai: The Rise and Fall of a
Decadent City 1842-1949** by Stella Dong
(HarperCollins)

WEBSITES
Art
www.duolunmoma.org
www.mocashanghai.org
www.shanghaimuseum.net
Design
sdb.sstec.com.cn
Newspaper
www.shanghaidaily.com
Magazine
shanghai.urbanatomy.com

COST OF LIVING
**Taxi from Pudong International
Airport to Fuxing Park**
¥155
Cappuccino
¥30
Packet of cigarettes
¥8
Daily newspaper
¥1
Bottle of champagne
¥360

SHANGHAI
Area
740 sq km
Population
20 million
Currency
Renminbi
Telephone codes
China: 86
Shanghai: 21
Time
GMT +8

AVERAGE TEMPERATURE / °C

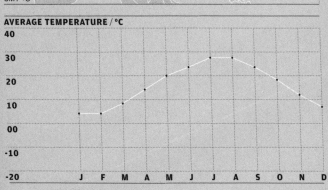

AVERAGE RAINFALL / MM

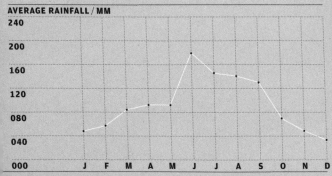

NEIGHBOURHOODS

THE AREAS YOU NEED TO KNOW AND WHY

To help you navigate the city, we've chosen the most interesting districts (see below and the map inside the back cover) and colour-coded our featured venues, according to their location; those venues that are outside these areas are not coloured.

JINGAN

Business appointments might take you to Nanjing Xilu, an artery of white-collar Shanghai. Here you will find glass-and-steel office towers and lager-fuelled bar strips, as well as John Portman's Shanghai Centre (1376 Nanjing Xilu, T 6279 8600), home of The Portman Ritz-Carlton (see p016). To the north is the Wusong River, a belt of sagging old industry and bohemian resettlement.

XINTIANDI

This olde-worlde mall of boutiques and eateries, including T8 (see p056) and Pavillon Costes (House 17, Lane 181, Taicang Lu, T 5306 9988), helped teach the city's developers the market logic of restoration, albeit in a controversial way. The Ben Wood-designed Xintiandi wiped out the old *longtang* – the brick tenements unique to early 20th-century Shanghai – to put up new ones, displacing thousands of locals.

THE BUND

This riverfront strip is the legacy of the Opium Wars, built by the Brits and their allies along the arc of the Huangpu. The façades of that era that remain, mostly from the 1920s and 1930s, were the public face of the banking and nightlife centre of the concession. Party cadres and state banks have moved in, as have Western retailers, such as Armani and Cartier. Venues like Glamour Bar (see p054) make the most of the super views.

FRENCH CONCESSION

Concentrated in today's Xuhui, Luwan and Nanshi districts, this area was first marked off in 1849 (after the British and Americans had settled here, but before the Japanese arrived) and sprawled west from the old Chinese city. Huge swathes are now gone, but the character of 'Frenchtown' remains. Trendy cafés and designer boutiques, such as Cha Gang (see p078) and Asobio (see p073), add a hip feel.

PUDONG

Meaning 'east of the Huangpu', Pudong was mostly fishing villages until two decades ago. It now stands as a model of how a state-lubricated economic machine has wrought cityscapes out of mega-malls, office spires and development zones. But this is the only one with five-star hotels, an airport designed by Paul Andreu, the SWFC (see p013) and the Oriental Pearl TV Tower (see p010).

PEOPLE'S PARK

From the 1850s, this was Shanghai's hippodrome, the site of derbies and polo. Today, it is both the city's civic centre and a recreational and cultural hub, with the tripod-shaped Shanghai Art Museum (see p012), Arte Charpentier's Shanghai Grand Theatre (300 Renmin Dadao, T 6372 8702) and MOCA (see p034), set in an artificial lake. The stretch of Nanjing Donglu that leads to the Bund is Shanghai's rendition of a Chinese pedestrian arcade.

LANDMARKS

THE SHAPE OF THE CITY SKYLINE

Shanghai is by far the most rewarding city in China to cover by foot, but also one of the hardest. If you're used to axial lines and rectilinear grids, it will leave you spinning. Unlike Beijing, which khans and emperors plotted nearly a millennium ago, modern Shanghai began to emerge only in the past 160 years – it had too many masterminds and too little time to devise a master plan. Even today, travel guides break down the city in different ways. Important arteries include Beijing, Nanjing and Fuxing. The old city, west of the Huangpu River, is quartered by the two main *gaojia* (raised roads), Yan'an Lu, which runs from east to west, and Nanbei Lu, which literally means 'south to north', while Huaihai forms the spine of the French Concession. But where do the concessions end and the communists begin? You figure that out only as you move along – and therein lies the mystique.

Much of the major construction in Shanghai in the past decade has taken place in Pudong, including the skyscrapers Jin Mao Tower and SWFC (see p013). The city's smaller-scale contemporary architecture is no less ambitious, notably Z58 (see p031), designed by Kengo Kuma & Associates, and Hongkou, the 1933 building (see p065). Once the largest abattoir in the Far East, this arresting structure originally designed by British architects, is midway through conversion into a mixed-use complex.
For full addresses, see Resources.

Oriental Pearl TV Tower
Still the signature building of modern
Shanghai, oozing technocratic glam, the
1994 TV tower has morphed from eyesore
to emblem. Arriving years before the city
landed the 2010 World Expo, it's a hilarious
tourist folly, but a pleasant, if queasily
pink-tinged place for a Bloody Mary.
Or save the entrance fee and just
contemplate the night-time illuminations.
1 Century Avenue, T 5879 1888

Shanghai Art Museum

This institution will never be the Met in New York, but since it launched in this building in 2000 it has become one of China's more progressive state museums. It hosts the Biennale (shanghaibiennale.com), and the permanent collection on the third floor offers an interesting, if tame, round-up of 20th-century Chinese painting. British architects Moorhead & Halse were the designers of this eclectic edifice, which opened in 1933 as the home of the Shanghai Race Club. Punters in their derby hats, mandarins with their braided cues – all came in their thousands to sit in the grandstands that overlooked the hippodrome, now People's Park (see p014). The four-faced clock under the bell tower was once dubbed 'Little Ben'. *325 Nanjing Xilu, T 6327 2829, sh-artmuseum.org.cn*

SWFC

At 492m, Pudong's 2008 Shanghai World Financial Center (SWFC) nips in just behind the 509m Taipei 101 skyscraper in Taiwan in the rankings of Asia's tallest buildings. Designed by Kohn Pedersen Fox, the tower was initially capped by a circular void, but the shape was changed to a trapezoid after rumblings that the original design was too strong an echo of Japan's rising sun emblem. Inside, its 101 storeys house the Park Hyatt hotel (see p023), offices, shops and an observation deck at the dizzying 474m mark. However, Skidmore, Owings & Merrill's adjacent Jin Mao Tower (T 5047 6688), completed in 1999, was the building that stamped Pudong as Shanghai's business district, its intricate exterior detailing taking its cue from a traditional Chinese pagoda.
100 Century Avenue, swfc-shanghai.com

People's Park

Before Beijing's architectural route march towards the 2008 Olympics, Jean-Marie Charpentier's Grand Theatre (T 6372 8702), here in People's Park, was the high point of China's East meets West frenzy. If it seems rather quaint now, when heavy hitters such as Lord Foster, Herzog & de Meuron and Rem Koolhaas have become involved in rebuilding the capital, the theatre did at least demonstrate the redemptive power of modern architecture, restoring People's Park to its rightful position as Shanghai's recreational and cultural heart, including venues such as MOCA and the Urban Planning Exhibition Center (see p034). The park itself has become a natural starting point for walking tours, which head past the shops of Nanjing Donglu onto the Bund, then over to the high-rises of Pudong.

HOTELS
WHERE TO STAY AND WHICH ROOMS TO BOOK

To be Shanghai or to see Shanghai? Many of the city's luxury hotels force you to choose. For the best Bund panoramas, park yourself in Pudong. The Park Hyatt (see po23) and Pudong Shangri-La (see po21) are without question *the* places to entertain with a view. The fast development on this side of the river has also spawned an outposts of The Ritz-Carlton, a W Hotel is slated, in 2012.

Across the Huangpu, The Portman Ritz-Carlton (1376 Nanjing Xilu, T 6279 8888) has stood as an international concession unto itself since the 1990s, while the Four Seasons (500 Weihai Lu, T 6256 8888) is still the gold standard in town. In Xintiandi and the Bund, several large-scale hotel ventures, such as a Conrad (99 Madang Lu, T 6386 9888), Jumeirah Hantang (88 Songshan Lu, T 6387 7888) and The Peninsula (32 Zhongshan Dong Yilu, T 2327 2888), which will house a multitude of rooftop restaurants and bars overlooking the river, launched recently.

Competition has pushed the hotel scene in a more design-led direction, with the Urbn (see po25) being the shining light. The Jia (see po28) follows closely behind. For a bargain, reserve a room at No 9 (9 Lane 355, Jianguo Xilu, T 6471 9950), a B&B housed in a refurbished mansion. Newly opened, on the south Bund, we also recommend checking in to the 19-room Waterhouse (opposite), designed by local firm Neri & Hu Design and Research Office. *For full addresses and room rates, see Resources.*

Waterhouse

Singaporean hotelier Loh Lik Peng (of The New Majestic and Wanderlust in Singapore) has transformed a 1930s factory in the Huangpu River dockyards into an industrial-glam, 19-room, boutique pad. Local architects Neri & Hu fuse the gritty factory framework (steel supports, concrete walls) with sleek architectural adaptions, topped off with an impressive collection of designer furnishings (Arne Jacobsen, Hans Wegner) and latest tech gizmos. Each of the bright white and wood rooms has a slightly different layout; we like Bund Suite 32 where you can gaze at the river junks and ferries from your bathtub. Table No 1 serves mod-Mediterranean fare by Michelin-starred Brit chef Jason Atherton.

1-3 Maojiayuan Lu, Zhongshan Nan Lu, T 6080 2988, www.waterhouseshanghai.com

Bund Junior Suite, Waterhouse

Tomorrow Square

A thrusting space rocket overlooking People's Park, Tomorrow Square was designed by architects John Portman & Associates and occupies the upper part of a 60-storey complex that includes apartments and commercial space.

It may be a Marriott, but there are some noteworthy touches, in particular the 38th-floor lobby, the marquetry in the cocktail bar and the enormous windows in all the rooms, which have sills big enough to sit on. As well as jaw-dropping views, guests can enjoy a swim in either the indoor or outdoor pools, before being buffed and beautified in the Mandara Spa.

399 Nanjing Xilu, T 5359 4969, www.marriott.com

Pudong Shangri-La

In late 2005, the Shangri-La opened an extension, Tower Two, to complement its huge Tower One. Designed by Kohn Pedersen Fox, the result is the Bund as cinema, as vast partitioned windows maximise the vistas. Bilkey Llinas Design did most of the interiors, as in the Executive Room (above), conceiving them so that you can shower while watching traders' junks slip by below. Adam Tihany clad the top-floor restaurant, Jade on 36, with such visual hors d'œuvres as oversized snuff boxes, while the in-house Japanese restaurant Nadaman is dark and slick. Bodily beautification comes courtesy of the Chi spa (T 5877 1503). The hotel is still mired in the sterility of Pudong, but this expanded complex acts as a buffer.
33 Fu Cheng Lu, T 6882 8888,
www.shangri-la.com

Park Hyatt

In a city of superlatives, what was once the highest hotel in the world, the Grand Hyatt, has been usurped by the Park Hyatt, spanning floors 79 to 93 of the 101-storey SWFC (see p013). Guests are whisked via express elevator to the 87th-floor lobby, which looks down on all around it, including the Jin Mao Tower (see p013). The hotel has just about everything you could want in one building, including a spa (left) and three restaurants, among them 100 Century Avenue (see p060). The 174 guest rooms have been given a modern Asian décor by New York-based interior designer Tony Chi; for the best 180-degree views, book one facing the river and the Bund, such as the Chairman Suite (above).
100 Century Avenue, T 6888 1234,
www.shanghai.park.hyatt.com

Urbn

Billed as the world's first carbon-neutral hotel when it opened in 2008, Urbn was designed by Shanghai architects AOO, and uses recycled materials and buys carbon credits to offset its energy use. We like the Studio Lounges (pictured) with the sunken tubs. The hotel offers t'ai chi and yoga classes.
183 Jiaozhou Lu, T 5153 4600, www.urbnhotels.com

The PuLi Hotel and Spa

Taking up 26 floors of the 2008 Park Place complex, The PuLi opened in early 2009. In the 229 rooms and suites, dragon-scaled screens, brass incense burners, ornate bronze mirrors and other antique-inspired pieces dot the otherwise sparse, neutral décor, like the lobby (above), created by the Australian-based Layan Design Group. Book one of the 61 rooms, such as the Grand Room, and suites on the Club Floors, which come with butler service and access to The Club Lounge, where you can enjoy spectacular city views over breakfast on its outdoor patio. Another draw is the PuLi's impressive Anantara Spa, which features a 25m infinity pool. Treatments, as you'd expect, are top-notch and Asian-tinged.
1 Changde Lu, T 3203 9999,
www.thepuli.com

Ritz-Carlton

High above the bustling Lujiazui financial district, Shanghai's second Ritz-Carlton crowns the top 18 floors of the 58-storey IFC South Tower (downstairs is a luxury shopping mall and metro station). Richard Farnell's opulent, contemporary interiors reference Shanghai's beloved 1930s art deco era, complete with polished chrome detailing, embossed murals and crimson stingray-skin lifts. Book the Bund-facing rooms for staggering views from the bed and claw-footed bathtub; and don't miss a paddle in the 53rd-floor pool. Of the four restaurants, the Super Potato-designed Flair on the 58th floor is the highlight – China's highest alfresco restaurant affords unforgettable views of the Bund and Oriental Pearl Tower from its huge terrace. *Shanghai IFC, 8 Century Ave, Pudong, T 2020 1888, www.ritzcarlton.com*

Jia

Ever since Singaporean Yenn Wong opened her first Jia hotel, designed by Philippe Starck, in Hong Kong in 2003, her boutique establishments have become hotly anticipated. The Shanghai sequel, opened in 2008, does not disappoint, though it makes do without Stark's input. Instead, Wong's design coterie included Melbourne's Hecker Phelan & Guthrie Interiors and BURO Architecture + Interiors, who did the rooms, and André Fu of Hong Kong firm AFSO, who created the lobby (right). The 55 rooms are pure pleasure, with Jia's trademark 'homeyness' concept manifest in the sofa areas and kitchenettes. All of the larger accommodations, such as the Penthouse Plus (above), have their own living room, and the two Penthouse suites are stylishly swanky, with their B&B Italia couches and Gio Ponti chairs.
931 West Nanjing Lu, T 6217 9000, www.jiashanghai.com

Z58
This stunning HQ of the Zhongtai Lighting Group was designed by Kengo Kuma & Associates. Features include a four-storey water-trickling atrium wall, two floors of offices, a ground-floor event space and two of the sleekest rooms in the city (pictured) on the fourth floor, adjacent to a club-like bar and a gym. They are mostly reserved for VIPs.
58 Panyu Lu, T 5258 2763, www.z58.org

24 HOURS

SEE THE BEST OF THE CITY IN JUST ONE DAY

Some Shanghai expats will tell you there's nothing to do here besides eat and drink. But this is the most open, cosmopolitan city in China, so there's a lot happening besides starry chefs opening restaurants on the Bund and socialites turning villas into clubs. Shanghai's cultural commissars, once the most reactionary in the land, have at last figured out how much the arts can boost the city's cachet. First came the Duolun Museum of Modern Art (27 Duolun Lu, T 6587 5996) in 2003, then MOCA (see p034) in 2005. Both had difficult starts, with the departure of major curators, but have since been working hard at reinvention. The design scene is more encouraging. A spin-off of the successful London fair, 100% Design Shanghai, which launched in 2008, joins Shanghai International Creative Industry Week to spark seven days of design-related activities held every autumn.

Our day takes you through Shanghai's most vibrant districts. Start at the centre of the action, in People's Park, with a tour of MOCA and the Urban Planning Exhibition Center (see p034), heading to Noodle Bull (see p035) for lunch, followed by the newly reopened Rockbund Art Museum (see p036). And to wrap, we head to two of the most sophisticated imports to hit the city recently – the sleek Lan Club (see p038) for dinner and, later on the achingly hip club Drop (see p039) for stylish cocktails.

For full addresses, see Resources.

09.00 Downstairs with David Laris

On the ground floor of eco-boutique Urbn hotel (see p024), and spilling out into the high-walled courtyard, this relaxed diner presided over by Australian chef David Laris reflects Urbn's sustainable philosophy in its fresh flavours, locally sourced ingredients and organic wine list. Seasonal meals on the mod-Mediterranean menu include monkfish with olive caponata, and red wine braised beef cheek with sweet peas. The stylishly rustic interiors feature repurposed timber floorboards and a wall of rusty woks. But the real winner is the cute, open-air courtyard – a great place to start the day with wholesome breakfasts and strong java served from 6.30am.
1st floor, URBN Hotel, 183 Jiaozhou Lu, T 5172 1300, www.urbnhotels.com

11.00 MOCA

Ever since its launch, Shanghai's Museum of Contemporary Art (MOCA) has been more notable for its location – in a man-made lake in the middle of People's Park (see p014) – than for its pedestrian, Euro-centric exhibitions. That is changing, and the idea going forward is for the museum's emphasis to shift firmly towards local artists. The plan is to put together a permanent collection that reflects the established Shanghai scene, and to showcase emerging talent. For a glimpse into the Shanghai of the future, head next to the compelling Urban Planning Exhibition Center (T 6372 2077), which offers visions of the city circa 2020. *231 Nanjing Xilu, T 6327 1282, www.mocashanghai.org*

13.00 Noodle Bull

There's no shortage of noodle joints in Shanghai, but this one is a cut above the rest. Created by the folks behind Spin ceramics (see p076) and Shintori restaurant (see p040), Noodle Bull's minimalist concrete interiors, long communal benches and simple scrolled menu tick all the boxes for a smart, swift luncheon. Hand-pulled soup and stir-fried noodles and Chinese-style tapas are served in large Spin bowls by ninja-like waiters. These are washed down with home-made, spiced plum juice and a small selection of beers and cocktails. All reasonably priced.

1st floor, A Mansion, 291 Fumin Lu,
T 6170 1299

15.00 Rockbund Art Museum

The 1932 art deco building that houses the new Rockbund Art Museum has a highly cultured pedigree. It was originally the headquarters of the Royal Asiatic Society, and the site was also used as a museum and public library. Reopened in 2010, David Chipperfield has restored the striking heritage façade and art deco interior detailing, while converting the venue into a hi-tech showpiece for contemporary Chinese art and creative exchange. The museum hosts exhibitions and art workshops in its atrium-linked spaces, while breaks are enjoyed at the terrace café. This is the first of 11 heritage buildings that David Chipperfield Architects is transforming behind the Bund.
20 Huqiu Lu, T 3310 9985,
www.rockbundartmuseum.org

20.00 Lan Club

After the success of Chinese restaurateur Zhang Lan's Philippe Starck-designed Lan Club in Beijing, a move to Shanghai was on the cards. This renovated Beaux Arts building a block away from the Bund dispenses with Starck's interior quirks in favour of the more strait-laced approach of French duo Patrick Gilles and Dorothée Boissier, who masterminded Buddakan in New York with Christian Liaigre. Their regal if somewhat funky Chinese-meets-French-colonial style adorns a Chinese restaurant on the first floor, a tapas bar on the second level, a private dining room (above) on the third floor, and above that an eaterie helmed by chef William Mahi. *102 Guangdong Lu, T 6323 8029, www.southbeautygroup.com*

22.00 Drop

The Shanghai outpost of DJ Joel Lai's hip Hong Kong club, Drop brings its proven formula of top international DJs, highly selective door policy and stylish late-night lounging to Shanghai's Bund. Behind the heritage façade, interiors by Italian Oobiq Architects are an opulent mix of Moorish mosaics, bold metallics, huge chandeliers and red Chesterfield sofas. Sculpturally pixilated reproductions of classic artworks line the walls, reflecting the subversive glamour of the crowd that packs into the intimate venue to enjoy yakitori skewers and watermelon martinis, while grooving to acid jazz, soul, garage and funky house. Stars and socialites huddle in the two VIP rooms, which resound to the popping of 'Chandelier' Champagnes (above).
55 Yuan Ming Yuan Lu, T 6329 1373, www.drop-shanghai.com

URBAN LIFE

CAFÉS, RESTAURANTS, BARS AND NIGHTCLUBS

A night out in Shanghai is an event like nowhere else in China and needs a little planning. Dinner reservations are de rigueur, and at some of the most popular clubs, VIP couches require pre-booking and carry a minimum tab of as much as ¥1,150. At places like Bar Rouge (see p055), where you can lounge on love seats or furry platform beds, this means the watchers are separated from the watched. Cabaret (6 Zhongshan Dong Yilu, T 6329 7333) and M2 (1266 Nanjing Lu, T 6288 6222) – for dancing – are two of our other favourite after-hours haunts, and for an elegant evening out, head to the Kee Club (see p051) in the French Concession, or if you want something raunchier, Gosney & Kallman's Chinatown (471 Zhapu Lu, T 6258 2078). Or try MiNT (see p043), which opened in 2009.

For travellers with a hankering for some Shanghainese cuisine, there's no shortage of affordable food served in old châteaux. One institution is Jesse's (41 Tianping Lu, T 6282 9260), but you should also eat at 1221 (1221 Yan'an Xilu, T 6213 6585). A recent trend is the fashion for smaller, Japanese-style bars – the industrial chic and menu at Shintori (803 Julu Lu, T 5404 5252) is perennially popular. And if you want to shun the clubs for a quieter late-night scene, head to the west French Concession and bars like Ci5 (1797 Huaihai Zhonglu, T 6471 8060), Kiitos (127 Yongfu Lu, T 6431 3787) and Bar Constellation No 2 (33 Yongjia Lu, T 5465 5993).

For full addresses, see Resources.

Café Sambal

Popular Beijing-based restaurateur Cho Chong Gee has expanded his much-loved Café Sambal to Shanghai, where it is one of the few Malaysian restaurants in town. Accessed via a long lane it forms part of the delightful eco dining enclave known as Jiashan Market. Sculptural interiors in dark granite, bare brick and warm woods set the tone, as does the aroma of Southeast Asian spices, that hits you as you enter through the heavy wooden door. The menu of mod-Malaysian crowd-pleasers – otak-otak fish cakes, oxtail soup, beef rendang, is accompanied by a long list of wines and cocktails. The second storey seating is a fine place for drinks, or step outside to the sunken terrace when the weather is warm. *37A, Jiashan Market, Lane 550 Shaanxi Nan Lu, T 3368 9529, www.cafesambal.com*

M1NT

If you're looking for Shanghai's biggest, loudest club, head here. The 2,500 sq m space on the top floor of a 24-storey office building near the Bund caters for a lively, champagne-swilling crowd, and the 17m-long shark tank makes quite a statement. It's a private club but non-members are welcome if it's not full.
24th floor, 318 Fuzhou Lu, T 6391 3191, www.m1nt.com.cn

Yè Shanghai

In an area where blandness prevails, Yè Shanghai offers stylish local cuisine in a surprisingly inventive interior. Situated in the theme-park entertainment area of Xintiandi, this should be one of Shanghai's duller offerings (like so many of its neighbours), but it is actually an impressive conversion of an old lanes house that serves consistently good food. The name means 'Shanghai nights',

but this is definitely a better bet for lunch. The smaller room on the upper floor, which can be hired for private dining, has vistas across the tiled roof on two sides. Host your farewell lunch here before you head out of town. *338 Huang Pi Nanlu, T 6311 2323, www.elite-concepts.com*

Whampoa Club

The first distinctly Chinese venture on the Bund, original chef Jereme Leung's Whampoa Club remains a super-stylish affair. Designed by Hong Kong-based Alan Chan, the wall of the reception chamber, carved in red and cream wood, shows two fleshy men in sumo stances and a geisha as referee. A long, mirrored hallway leads to the dining room, where servers in silk tops buzz around, though no one person seems to be in charge (very Chinese). Then come incumbent chef Yappoh Weng's Shanghainese dishes, simply done with a few twists: tea-smoked eggs, chilled drunken chicken, chrysanthemum-shaped spring rolls and osmanthus-candied lotus root filled with slow-cooked grains. *5th floor, Three on the Bund, 3 Zhongshan Dong Yilu, T 6321 3737, www.threeonthebund.com*

Lune

For unpretentious drinking, dancing and DJs, take the comically tiny elevator to the fourth floor where you'll find youthful neighbourhood lounge Lune behind padded swing doors. Lune's wildly patterned, retro design (hello disco ball) is a little downbeat around the edges, but that suits the laidback crowd that comes here to chill with friends on large zigzag striped sofas and gyrate to a soundtrack of house, jazz, funk, down-beat and soul spun by guest DJs. American bar bites accompany a straightforward and well-priced drinks list. Regular weekly events focus on different music styles, with the occasional live act taking the stage.
4th floor, 218 Xinle Lu, T 139 0197 4330

Maison Pourcel

It's fitting that the Michelin-starred Pourcel twins from France chose the historic Hong Fangzi (Red House) in the French Concession as the location for their latest Shanghai restaurant; the original Hong Fangzi was China's most famous French dining institution. The Pourcel's 50-seat dining room in a glass rooftop pavilion is one of Shanghai's most romantic, with dove-grey armchairs and art deco lamps surrounded by wraparound vistas of Shanghai's rooftops. Jacques Pourcel can regularly be found in the kitchen preparing elaborate, Mediterranean-influenced French dishes. For a less pricey sampler, the art deco styled sixth-floor cocktail lounge is a classy place to sip from the 3,000-bottle wine list. *6th and 8th floors, 35 Shanxi Nan Lu, T 6215 8777, www.maisonpourcel.com*

Kee Club

On the two top floors of the restored 796 Huaihai Lu building, which also includes Dunhill Villas (see p072), the members-only Kee Club is the hotly anticipated Shanghai outpost of the Hong Kong venue of the same name. Founded in 2001 by Austrian Christian Rhomberg and his wife, Maria, the Hong Kong Kee has upheld its status as a high-society hangout, while the smaller Shanghai branch promises to be more democratic, opening to non-members for an initial period. Visit the swanky bar, filled with leather Chesterfields and Arne Jacobsen 'Egg' chairs (left), or book a table in the dining room (above), which serves fine French cuisine. Given a day's notice, the kitchen can also serve Chinese fare.
3rd and 4th floors, 796 Huaihai Zhonglu, T 3395 0888, www.keeclub.com

Xibo

A stylish alternative to the usually
flamboyant Xinjiang style, Xibo offers
traditional northwestern Xinjiang fare
in a comfortable chic environment.
Run by Xibonese restaurateur Anita
Kuo, the menu, is authentic, with Uighur
standards – lamb, cumin, flat breads
– plus a range of regional specialities
from Xibo, Kazakstan and even Russia.
3rd floor, 83 Changshu Lu, T 5403 8330

Glamour Bar

M on the Bund is still *the* spot for a cocktail-fuelled weekend brunch with an unrivalled river panorama. But if it's evening fun you're after, head straight to Glamour Bar, located one floor below M. Though the Shanghai deco style may be ubiquitous in this part of the city, designers Debra Little and Roger Hackworth have realised the theme particularly well here, with hand-painted Chinese murals and plenty of mirrors thoughtfully provided for the preeners who flock here for a nightcap.
6th floor, 5 Zhongshan Dong Yilu, T 6350 9988, www.m-restaurantgroup.com

Bar Rouge

Large photographic prints, mirrored walls, billowy silk drapes and modern furniture bridge the gaps between Europe and China in this ever popular bar, located in the temple to luxury-goods retailing and fine dining that is the Bund 18 development. A crowd of local entrepreneurs, their international guests and harried refugees from the shops below might not make for an especially fascinating scene, but Rouge remains a relatively sophisticated option in a place that you are certain to pass through at least once during your stay.
7th floor, 18 Zhongshan Dong Yilu,
T 6339 1199, www.bar-rouge-shanghai.com

T8 Restaurant & Bar
Rather than pandering to the retro
temptations of its Xintiandi environs,
T8 focuses on fusing new flavours for
its high-powered clientele, and the result
is a standout restaurant among the well-
trafficked eateries of the entertainment
district. Chill out on one of the windowside
sofas, tucked between the latticework
screens, Cosmopolitan in hand, and order
a dish or two from the open kitchen.
The menu, which has been reinterpreted
by a series of chefs in the past few years,
changes frequently, but expect to find
staples such as beef carpaccio, foie gras
crème brûlée and tataki of sesame-
crusted tuna. If you can squeeze it in,
finish with T8's infamous Chocolate
Addiction platter or the wickedly good
warm apple tart with caramel.
8 Xintiandi Beilu, Lane 181, Taicang Lu,
T 6355 8999, www.t8shanghai.com

The Apartment

A smattering of eclectic armchairs, low tables, bare brick walls and a drum set in the corner – The Apartment feels like a house party at a friend's funky New York loft, except that the old warehouse windows look out over the leafy canopy of Shanghgai's lanes. A modish crowd kicks back over wood-fired gourmet pizzas and a wide array of well-mixed martinis and boutique beers. A comforting menu of sharable entrees by popular chef Sean Jorgensen is also available throughout the lounge and in the adjoining dining room. Don't miss the rooftop deck with its own bar, pizza kitchen and magical views of the French Concession.
3rd floor, 47 Yongfu Lu, 6437 9478, www.theapartment-shanghai.com

Jean Georges

Architect Michael Graves fused elements of Parisian cabaret and Oriental bordello, with a touch of clubby masculinity. The materials fit the mood: dark walnut flooring, copper-leafed ceilings and eel-skin furniture in the champagne bar, and velvet drapes adding some slink to the dining area. The menu, from chef Jean-Georges Vongerichten, features dishes like sea scallops with cauliflower and a 'caper-resin' emulsion. The food alone is almost enough to distract diners from the 180-degree views of the Bund.
4th floor, Three on the Bund,
3 Zhongshan Dong Yilu, T 6321 7733,
www.threeonthebund.com

100 Century Avenue

If the SWFC (see p013) is a city within a city, the restaurant complex at the Park Hyatt (see p023) is a culinary metropolis in itself. On the top three floors below the SWFC observatory, the restaurant and bar cluster dishes up Chinese, Japanese and Western cuisine, via wood-fired ovens, an oyster bar and a sushi station, and boasts impressive art installations – and that's just on the first floor (above). One level up is a jazz-age lounge bar, with dance floor and ballroom dancing events several nights a week, and martinis served in 50cm-high glasses. Don't feel like mingling? Book a private dining space on the third level. And yes, being almost 500m up will definitely make you feel on top of it all. *91st to 93rd floors, Park Hyatt, SWFC, 100 Century Avenue, T 6888 1234, www.shanghai.park.hyatt.com*

INSIDER'S GUIDE
JIANG QIONG ER, ARTISTIC DIRECTOR

Jiang Qiong'er is the creative Chinese spirit behind Hermes'
new luxury Oriental brand, Shang Xia (see p074). Born into
a Shanghainese family of artists-creators (her father Xing Tonghe
was the architect of the Shanghai Museum), Jiang started painting
at the age of two and studied in Paris, before returning to Shanghai
and devoting herself to reviving China's rich design heritage. For
Shanghai's favourite snack, pouch-shaped *xiaolongbao* dumplings,
Jiang heads to Din Tai Fung (Shop 11A, Building 6, Xintiandi South
Block, T 6385 8378). She loves veteran Shanghainese haunt 1931
(112 Maoming Nan Lu, T 6472 5264), a vintage-style parlour where
'the food and service are consistently great'. For international
dining, she likes Issimo (931 West Nanjing Road, T 6287 9009) for
its Mediterranean flavours and design flair. The lobby of the PuLi
(1 ChangDe Road, T 3203 9999) hotel is her pick for cocktails.

To witness the cutting-edge of modern Chinese art, Jiang heads
to the gallery district at Moganshan Lu or Huaihai Lu's Sculpture
Space. The former abattoir turned creative hub, 1933 (see p065), is
a must for its architectural drama. 'Lose yourself in the streets
around the French Concession, and you'll find an endless supply
of gems. A box of matchsticks, Chinese snacks, silk slippers, fresh
tea leaves – the best souvenirs are those that capture authentic
local culture and a precious moment of personal discovery.'
For full addresses, see Resources.

ARCHITOUR
A GUIDE TO SHANGHAI'S ICONIC BUILDINGS

The old Shanghai was a traditional walled city, encircled by what are now the roads Renmin Lu and Zhonghua Lu, with the 16th-century Yuyuan Garden as its centrepiece. The foreign treaty port, by contrast, spread colourfully all around it, like a painter's palette. By the 20th century, these two architectural bloodlines had already begun to intermingle, but this was long before the construction of Pudong on the east side of the Huangpu, with its endlessly anodyne local take on the skyscraper, the notable exception being SOM's Jin Mao Tower (see p009).

As far back as the 1930s, city planners had created swathes of *longtang*, rows of brick houses similar to the terraced streets in European towns, but with maze-like passages within, which are patently Chinese. Catch these before they disappear as, since the 1990s, many have been bulldozed to clear premium real estate for the city's new towers. Many of the villas have gone too – even IM Pei could not save a family mansion. But for all their faults, and the relentless pace of urbanisim here, local developers have been more reverential than in most Chinese cities, recultivating some of Shanghai's urban roots, especially around Suzhou Creek, the French Concession and the Bund. Today, its rapidly changing streetscapes continue to offer the thrill of watching the city's interaction with the West – and it's all still in flux.

For full addresses, see Resources.

1933

This former abbatoir, named after its completion date and designed by British architects, is one of the most dramatic and idiosyncratic buildings in Shanghai. Following a massive restoration to transform it into a buzzy cultural and commerical hub, it will house an event space, restaurants and a clutch of stores, including local ceramicists Asianera. In essence, the building is an ornate concrete shell, with cavernous and low-slung spaces, bridges and staircases creating an Escher-esque interior. A concrete screen with carved art deco designs forms the façade. Paul Liu, ex-executive director of Three on the Bund, has been working with chef David Laris on the project. Progress is slow, but look out for new eateries.
10 Shajing Lu, Hongkou, T 6501 1933, www.1933-shanghai.com

Chinese Pavilion

Shanghai's 'Eiffel Tower' – dubbed the 'Crown of the East' – was built to house the China National Pavilion at the Shanghai World Expo 2010. The $220 million inverted pyramid stands 63m tall and is heavily imbued with cultural symbolism. Painted seven shades of 'China red', its large overhanging roof is constructed with traditional interlocking wooden brackets, called *dougong*; the 56 *dougong* represent China's 56 ethnic minorities. From above, the rooftop grid pattern is laid out like an ancient Chinese city, and the *diezhuan* calliagraphy across the exterior reflects that used on official stamps. Its exhibition of cultural relics and installations has been extended until 31 May 2011, after which it will be converted into an events space. *Pudong Nan Lu by Shangnan Lu, T 2020 2010, cp.expo2010.cn*

Qingpu

Who said that China's urban planners don't plan? Qingpu, a 5,000-year-old water town located one hour outside Shanghai, is expanding rapidly into a satellite city – the population already exceeds 460,000 – driven here by the growth of light manufacturing and affordable apartment blocks. In 2002, Qingpu's then vice district chief, Jiwei Sun, began courting top foreign and native architects, offering them little money, but a lot of creative freedom. Spanish firm Sancho Madridejos created a geometric wonder of a church. The Chinese firm Atelier Deshaus designed modernist cube-based buildings, including the colourful Xiayu Kindergarten, while the Chinese architect Qingyun Ma designed Thumb Island (pictured), a community centre.

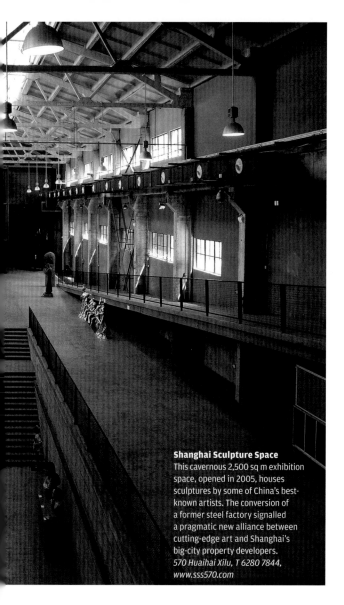

Shanghai Sculpture Space
This cavernous 2,500 sq m exhibition space, opened in 2005, houses sculptures by some of China's best-known artists. The conversion of a former steel factory signalled a pragmatic new alliance between cutting-edge art and Shanghai's big-city property developers.
570 Huaihai Xilu, T 6280 7844, www.sss570.com

SHOPPING

THE BEST RETAIL THERAPY AND WHAT TO BUY

Think of today's Shanghai as a catwalk: the world's top brands strutting into the domestic market; homegrown talent marching out to meet the West's gaze. What is special in this city is when the two meet. Xintiandi's alleys yield the big names in Chinese fashion, Shanghai Tang and Vivienne Tam, but for bold cross-cultural remixes, check out the stores in the French Concession, like Wang Yiyang's Cha Gang (see p078) and Nest (see p079). The latter is the new face of Taikang Lu, which is morphing from a corridor of trinket shops into a zone of more sophisticated retail concepts.

Many shops in the French Concession are responding to the increasing demand for more grown-up menswear, led by the new Dunhill flagship (796 Huaihai Zhonglu, T 3395 0810), located in a French-style villa. Antique-hunters should make a beeline for Dongtai (Dongtai Lu) and Fuyu (Fangbang Zhonglu) markets, which sell an abundance of Concession-era treasures: Tiffany-style lamps, opium pipes and phonographs. For art collectors, the M50 (50 Moganshan Lu) zone is a one-stop shop. If you're on the Bund, skip the big brands in favour of the creative epiphanies Design Republic (see p077) and Suzhou Cobblers (Unit 101, 17 Fuzhou Lu, T 6321 7087). The South Bund Soft-Spinning Material Market (399 Lujiabang Lu, T 6377 2322) remains the most popular place to order local custom-made shirts and suits.

For full addresses, see Resources.

Asobio

Asobio's first storefront boutique is a spacious affair in the huge Channel One mall, to the north of downtown. Women and menswear is arranged over two separate floors linked by a curving staircase, with plate glass windows overlooking the street. A stitch above other fast fashion brands, Asobio's sparkling white- and charcoal-toned shop, designed by Japanese firm Nendo, riffs on the theme of focus using a finely veined leaf motif that appears across the floors and walls in various levels of magnification and exposure. Against the soft backdrop, clearest focus is reserved for the long racks of constantly updated, fashion-forward casual wear, footwear and accessories by this Italian brand, popular across China.
1st and 2nd floors, Channel One, 155 Changshou Lu, T 3131 5173, www.asobio.com

Shang Xia
Launched in 2010 and dedicated to its fastest-growing market, Hermès' new luxury brand Shang Xia (meaning 'up down' in Mandarin) presents a contemporary take on traditional Chinese design. The collections of home accessories and fashion is created by young Paris-trained designer Jiang Qiong'er (see p062).
T 6390 8899, www.shang-xia.com

Spin Ceramics

One of the best designed retail spaces in the city, Spin opened in 2004 and features some of the most convincing fusions of ancient Chinese craft and modern aesthetic. Opened by the owner of the Shintori and Peoples chains of restaurants and bars, the store literally 'spun off' in order to fill a gaping need for beautiful, reasonably priced objects. The collection ranges from chopstick holders and sculptural vases to serving trays and all creative manner of tableware, at prices starting as low as ¥20.

Building 3, 758 Julu Lu, T 6279 2545

Design Republic

Every city needs an emporium dedicated to the best contemporary design, and in Shanghai this is it. Founded and run by architects Lyndon Neri and Rossana Hu, the showroom looks more like an installation than a retail space. Since opening in 2006, Design Republic has hosted launches for Tom Dixon, Marcel Wanders and Moooi, and in just a few years has single-handedly made viewing contemporary design one of the main attractions of a visit to the Bund. As well as a strong collection from foreign designers, shoppers will find Neri & Hu's own line. Items include lacquered trays, double-walled glasses and the 'ZiSha' stacking tea set (above), ¥690, all of which are designed, sourced and produced locally.
1st floor, 5 Zhongshan Dong Yilu, T 6329 3123, www.thedesignrepublic.com

Cha Gang

Fashion designer Wang Yiyang has almost single-handedly transformed local apparel and accessory design. His store, Cha Gang, which moved from its previous location in the Fuxing Lu complex in March 2008, is a sparsely furnished white space that neatly showcases his graphic printed tees, as well as more avant-garde, chunky, padded, electric-blue bags and oversized knits. If you want a gift or a one-off piece, the shop also sells a range of idiosyncratic accessories, many of them updated versions of everyday household items. Indeed, the name of the shop itself means 'tea container'.

1st floor, 70 Yongfu Lu, T 6437 3104, www.chagang.cn

Nest

Less a store, more a design collective, Nest gathers together some of the city's most interesting locally made, environmentally sensitive products, from cardboard chairs by Shanghai-based architects AOO to organic children's clothing by Wobaby Basics. Created by Danish born Trine Targett, founder of the design brand Jooi, the store was part of her quest to modernise traditional Chinese objects

crafted by local artisans. The space, which is working towards becoming a leader in 'carbon neutral' retail destinations in China, also hosts 'Designer Talk Evenings'.
International Artist Factory, 2nd floor, Studio 201, Lane 210, Taikang Lu, T 6466 9524, www.nestshanghai.com

The Villa
A fashionista's fantasy styled like a boudoir, The Villa showcases hand-picked looks from 20 of the hottest US and European designers, many not available elsewhere in China. Cocktail wear and daytime attire from the likes of Hervé Léger, Proenza Schouler and Rebecca Minkoff are sectioned according to occasion and paired with adorable clutches, jewels and other one-of-a-kind accessories. Completing the experience, pretty changing rooms and vintage-style sofas are arranged between the racks for contemplating purchases with friends over a glass of bubbly or espresso – or depositing a male companion while you browse. The brainchild of The Villa, American expat, Sara Villarreal, who roams the globe in search of fashion pieces is usually on hand to offer style advice.
1 Taojiang Lu, T 6466 9322,
www.shopthevilla.com

Banmoo

Meaning 'half wood' in Chinese, Banmoo is the baby of Shanghai product designer Lv Yongzhong. Since opening in a small storefront in Xintiandi in 2006, Banmoo has since made the leap to this loft-like Changning location (left), which is better suited to showcasing its sculptural furniture. We're also fans of the tableware, especially the 'Carry moon' incense holder (above), ¥268. Other covetable items, such as the rosewood boxes for storing books, reveal Lv's penchant for handmade designs, while the 'Calligraphy' chair, resembling a Chinese character in profile, and made from laser-cut ribs of high-density fibreboard, exemplifies his melding of technology and cultural history.
1st floor, Building 1, No 12, Lane 1384 Wanhangdu Lu, Changning,
T 6128 5818, www.banmoo.cn

Song Fang Maison de Thé

In China, tea is both hallowed and taken for granted – tea shops often look too much like pharmacies – which is why Song Fang is such a gem. Set on the corner of a busy street in the French Concession, the store is named after the Chinese translation of its French owner's surname, Florence Samson. After working for luxury firms such as Veuve Clicquot and Christian Dior, Samson had the idea of creating a *maison de thé* selling some of the most exquisite leaves grown in China, such as oolong and pu'er from Wuyi and Fujian, plus French blends such as Pomme d'Amour (50g packs range from ¥80-¥790). Head up to the second or third floor to sip your chosen blend. Tasteful tea paraphernalia, including teapots (from ¥200-¥1,500), is also on sale.
227 Yongjia Lu, T 6433 8283

Feiyue shoes

Founded in the 1920s in Shanghai, this fabled trainer brand has been worn by numerous generations of Chinese children, becoming as commonplace in China as Keds or Vans in the US. A few years ago, Feiyue shoes, which cost ¥28, could be found in just about every corner shop or clothing retailer in Shanghai, and their cheapness and durability etched the name Feiyue, which means 'flying forward', into the memory of even the youngest Chinese. But licensing by a French group has led to the shoes becoming a cult brand abroad, and they are now much harder to find in their homeland. However, one Shanghai shop, the Feiyue Factory Store (T 6273 8847) at 585 Zunyi Lu, is rumoured to have links with the original factory, and this is where we recommend you go.

Aegis Shanghai
This handsomely curated collection of
men's contemporary designer clothes,
footwear and accessories, includes
several labels making their debut in
mainland China. Manly memorabilia
(vintage suitcases, radios) and bold
dark wood floorboards provide a
backdrop for the suave collections.
777 Julu Lu, T 5403 9869,
www.projectaegis.com

SPORTS AND SPAS
WORK OUT, CHILL OUT OR JUST WATCH

City strolling in China doesn't get much better than in Shanghai. The French Concession, the Bund and Suzhou Creek all offer rewarding walks. Jog at your own risk, though, preferably setting out in the early morning, before cars choke the streets. If you are staying on the *puxi* (west) side of the river, ask your concierge to map out a simple rectilinear route around the Bund and back. In Pudong, go running in Century Park, part of the city's vast new frontier. If you want to make new friends while you're at it, join Hash House Harriers, who run on Sundays (shanghai-hhh.com). Afterwards you'll need a foot massage, and podiatric options are omnipresent; look for signs of footprints. The Liangzi chain of shops, which has green signage, is reliable, or head to Green Massage (58 Taicang Lu, T 5386 0222) for an upscale version of classic local treatments. One of our favourite all-round spas is Super Sense (352 Ashun Lu, Hongqiao, T 6219 6553).

For golfers, there are courses galore. At the Riviera Golf Resort (277 Yangzi Lu, Jiading, T 5912 6888), just outside town, a round is ¥380. Further afield, the Silport Golf Club (Dian-Shan Lake, Kunshan Jiangsu, T 5748 1111) has 18 public holes set among lakes and rivers. To get some local energy flowing in your blood, shadow the t'ai chi practitioners in Fuxing Park or, at the weekend, join the retired couples waltzing and jitterbugging on the pavement. *For full addresses, see Resources.*

Banyan Tree Spa

By far the closest thing to an island paradise by the Bund, Banyan Tree's Shanghai outpost, located inside The Westin, is an Asian concept spa where both the décor and treatments are based on the Chinese philosophy of the five elements: earth balances, fire vitalises, and so on. Couples are attracted by the Yin Yang treatments in the two-table suites (above), which also have a hot tub. You should also try the 90-minute Balinese massage. Before each session here your feet are soaked and stroked in a basin with rose petals and oil is applied to the skin while you relax with a herbal tea.
3rd floor, The Westin, Bund Center,
88 Henan Zhonglu, T 6335 1888,
www.banyantreespa.com

The Peninsula Spa
Cocooned amid neo-classic décor, Peninsula's 1,250 sq m spa by ESPA offers luxurious tailored treatment in its seven treatment rooms and two VIP suites. After an hour or two of pampering, be sure to take a dip in the swimming pool (pictured), or alternatively order a light snack poolside. *32 Zhongshan Road, Huangpu, T 2327 6599, www.peninsula.com/Shanghai*

ESPA, Ritz-Carlton

This gem of a spa on the 55th floor of the new Ritz-Carlton Shanghai, Pudong is inspired by a jewellery box. Opalescent and crystal-cut, the day spa features 10 treatment rooms with skyline views, including a couple's Harmony Suite with its own window-side tub. Arrive well before your treatment to enjoy the complimentary crystal steam room, rock sauna and ice fountain. The spa menu, using all-natural ESPA products, includes localised specialties, like traditional Tui Na massage and a Jade Qi Yun full body treatment using jade rollers. Afterwards, relax in the spa lounge with tea and biscotti, while taking in the views of the Oriental Pearl Tower. *55th floor, Shanghai IFC, 8 Century Ave, Pudong, T 2020 1888, www.ritzcarlton.com*

Y+ Yoga Center

Hong Kong native Harry Yu has created a Taj Mahal of a yoga studio at Y+. Done out with a monastic motif, it is a series of bright white and pastel chambers set behind dark antique doors in a converted 1932 four-storey art deco villa. The original wood flooring remains, but the space has been opened up through the use of glass walls. Y+ runs classes from the early morning to the late evening in a mix of styles: 'Yin' (basic), flow, Bikram (37-40°C) and, most challenging of all, ashtanga. You can cool off afterwards on the roof, with a refreshing cucumber juice in hand. There is also a cutting-edge, flagship Y+ Yoga Center in Xintiandi (T 6340 6161), opposite the Fuxing Center, decorated by Lyndon Neri of NHDRO. *299-2 Fuxing Xilu, T 6433 4330, www.yplus.com.cn*

Evian Spa

Zen descends as soon as you step into Evian Spa's cathedral-like, 35m-high atrium, artfully studded with a Japanese rock garden across thick-pile jade carpet. The most dramatic and serene space in the Michael Graves designed Three on the Bund lifestyle complex, this is one of Shanghai's few luxury day spas outside of five-star hotels. Robed therapists guide spa-goers past channels of Evian water to the 14 individually themed treatment suites — we like the bamboo and mother-of-pearl rooms. The comprehensive spa menu covers everything from traditional Oriental treatments to hi-tech European beauty care and hydrotherapies. The adjacent men's salon, Barbers by Three, offers haircuts, facials and traditional Shanghainese pedicures.

3 Zhongshan Dong Lu, T 6321 6622,
www.threeonthebund.com

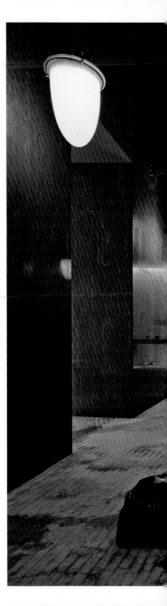

ESCAPES

WHERE TO GO IF YOU WANT TO LEAVE TOWN

Many people will tell you to hit the so-called 'earthly paradises' of Hangzhou (see p100) and Suzhou, and if time is of the essence, they are probably right. Suzhou, about an hour away by train, is the closer. Though yet to address its reform-era vices, namely a sleazy sex industry and ersatz architecture, the city offers the famous gardens of the imperial élite and a sail on the Grand Canal.

Further afield, south of Hangzhou, we recommend Moganshan, just under three hours by car from Shanghai. A retreat once popular with both expats and locals in the 1920s and 1930s, the area has made a comeback recently – media mogul Hong Huang renovated a house here that used to belong to her mother, while Naked Retreats (opposite) was a welcome accommodation addition in 2007. The Moganshan Lodge (Songliang Shanzhuang, Yin Shan Jie, T 0572 803 3011) is a good local café, and the mountains provide a beautiful setting for BBQs, hikes and communing with nature.

Alternatively, Chongming Island, 40 minutes from Shanghai by ferry, is predominantly a national park and nature reserve, home to many species of birds. A minimum of an hour and a half away by bus or car are six ancient Yangtze water towns: Zhouzhuang, Tongli and the 'Venetian canal' outposts of Luzhi, Nanxun, Wuzhen and Xitang, some of which are featured on UNESCO's World Heritage list. The towns have become trials in sustainable tourism.
For full addresses, see Resources.

Naked Retreats, Moganshan

Moganshan sits near the bamboo-forested Tianmu mountain. Naked Retreats, run by Grant Horsfield and Gabriela Lo, is a series of properties renovated by Delphine Yip, a partner at Ben Wood's architectural practice. Located in a village called 395, there are four bungalows, three studios and a communal house. An *ayi* (local helper) is available to cook the village-style cuisine *nong jia cai* at your retreat, while fully stocked kitchens ensure guests can also host their own dinners in this serene rustic setting.
*395 Village Moganshan, Wu Kang,
T 5465 9577, nakedretreats.cn*

Zhujiajiao

If you have only half a day to spare, this is a quick way to take in a sleepy water town. In just 45 minutes, you can be lingering at the 16th-century Fangsheng Bridge, the entrance to the present-day village, watching Chinese tourists toss goldfish and turtles into the river to save the creatures' lives and improve the fate of their own (*fangsheng* translates as 'freeing captive animals').

Fuchun Resort, Hangzhou
In Marco Polo's day, Hangzhou was a
cosmopolitan hub, and today it is showing
signs of becoming one again. West Lake,
in the town centre, remains one of
the loveliest green spaces in China,
notwithstanding the build-up of bar strips
and amusement arcades around parts
of it. Hangzhou boasts a couple of the
country's strongest art and literature
schools, including the China Academy of
Art, and these have coloured the town's
overall complexion. Style queen and
art collector Pearl Lam has now closed
Contrasts, her furniture and design
gallery here, but there's still lots to see
and plenty of high-end shopping down
the road. Outside town, Fuchun Resort
(right and overleaf) popped up in 2004,
hugging a lake on one side and tea
plantations on the other.
Hangfu Yanjiang Lu, Fuyang,
T 0571 6346 1111, fuchunresort.com

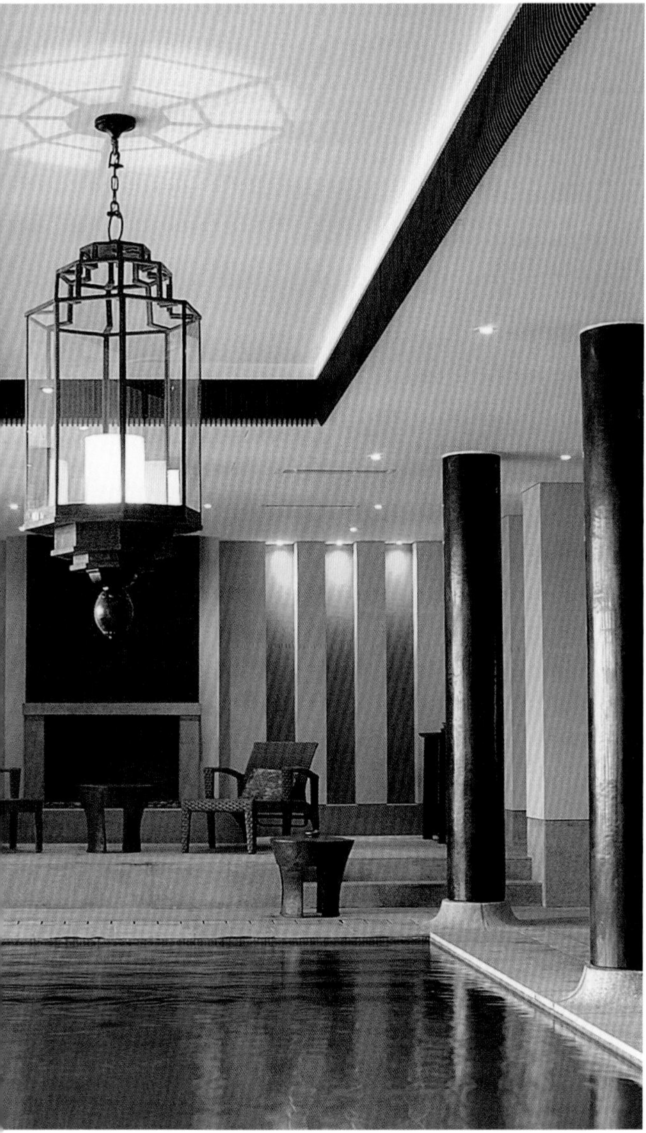

Fuchun Resort, Hangzhou

NOTES
SKETCHES AND MEMOS

RESOURCES

CITY GUIDE DIRECTORY

A

The Apartment 058
3rd floor
47 Youngfu Lu
T 6437 9478
www.theapartment-shanghai.com

Aegis Shanghai 086
777 Julu Lu
T 5403 9869
www.projectaegis.com

Asobio 073
1st and 2nd floors,
Channel One
155 Changshou Lu
T 3131 5173
www.asobio.com

B

Banmoo 083
1st floor
Building 1
No 12
Lane 1384
Wanhangdu Lu
Changning
T 6128 5818
www.banmoo.cn

Banyan Tree Spa 089
3rd floor
The Westin
Bund Center
88 Henan Zhonglu
T 6335 1888
www.banyantreespa.com

Bar Constellation No 2 040
33 Yongjia Lu
T 5465 5993

Bar Rouge 055
7th floor
18 Zhongshan Dong Yilu
T 6339 1199
www.bar-rouge-shanghai.com

C

Cabaret 040
6 Zhongshan Dong Yilu
T 6329 7333

Café Sambal 041
37 Jiashan Market
Lane 550 Shaanxi Nan Lu
T 3368 9529

Cha Gang 078
1st floor
70 Yongfu Lu
T 6437 3104
www.chagang.cn

Chi 021
6th floor
Pudong Shangri-La
33 Fu Cheng Lu
T 5877 1503
www.shangri-la.com

Ci5 040
1797 Huaihai Zhonglu
T 6471 8060

D

Design Republic 077
1st floor
5 Zhongshan Dong Yilu
T 6329 3123
www.thedesignrepublic.com

Dongtai market 072
Dongtai Lu

HOTELS
ADDRESSES AND ROOM RATES

Conrad 016
Room rates:
prices on request
99 Madang Lu
T 6386 9888
www.conradhotels1.hilton.com

Four Seasons 016
Room rates:
double, from ¥2,185
500 Weihai Lu
T 6256 8888
www.fourseasons.com/shanghai

Fuchun Resort 100
Room rates:
double, from ¥2,300
Hangfu Yanjiang Lu
Fuyang
Hangzhou
T 0571 6346 1111
www.fuchunresort.com

Jia 028
Room rates:
Studio, Studio Plus, from ¥2,600;
Balcony Suite, from ¥4,200;
Penthouse, ¥12,000;
Penthouse Plus, ¥18,000
931 West Nanjing Xilu
T 6217 9000
www.jiashanghai.com

Jumeirah Hantang 016
Room rates:
double, from ¥4,100
88 Songshan Lu
T 6387 7888
www.jumeirah.com

Naked Retreats 097
Room rates:
Purple Ridge, from ¥700 per person;
Studio, from ¥1,400;
Bamboo Bungalow, from ¥1,400
395 Village Moganshan
Wu Kang
T 5465 9577
www.nakedretreats.cn

No 9 016
Room rates:
double, from ¥1,200
9 Lane 355
Jianguo Xilu
T 6471 9950

Park Hyatt 023
Room rates:
double, from ¥2,600;
Chairman Suite, from ¥101,000
SWFC
100 Century Avenue
T 6888 1234
www.shanghai.park.hyatt.com

The Peninsula 016
Room rates:
prices on request
32 Zhongshan Dong Yilu
T 2327 2888
www.peninsula.com/shanghai

The Portman Ritz-Carlton 016
Room rates:
double, from ¥4,000
Shanghai Centre
1376 Nanjing Xilu
T 6279 8888
www.ritzcarlton.com/hotels/shanghai

Pudong Shangri-La 021
Room rates:
double, from ¥2,100;
Executive Room, from ¥2,400
33 Fu Cheng Lu
T 6882 8888
www.shangri-la.com

The PuLi Hotel and Spa 026
Room rates:
double, from ¥3,400;
Club rooms, from ¥4,200
1 Changde Lu
T 3203 9999
www.thepuli.com

Ritz-Carlton, Pudong 027
Room rates:
double, from ¥5,000
8 Century Avenue
T 2020 1888
www.ritzcarlton.com/hotels/shanghai

Tomorrow Square 020
Room rates:
double, from ¥1,400
399 Nanjing Xilu
T 5359 4969
www.marriott.com

Urbn 025
Room rates:
Studio Lounge, from ¥1,400;
Garden View Room, from ¥1,650;
Courtyard Suite, from ¥4,600;
Penthouse Suite, ¥8,000
183 Jiaozhou Lu
T 5153 4600
www.urbnhotels.com

Waterhouse 017
Room rates:
Junior Bund, from ¥1,700;
double, from ¥1,200
1-3 Maojiayuan Lu
T 6080 2988
www.waterhouseshanghai.com

Z58 031
Room rates:
double, ¥30,000
58 Panyu Lu
T 5258 2763
www.z58.org

WALLPAPER* CITY GUIDES

Editorial Director
Richard Cook

Art Director
Loran Stosskopf
Editors
Rachael Moloney
O'ar Pali
Authors
Jonathan Ansfield
Amy Fabris-Shi
Andrew Yang
Deputy Editor
Jeremy Case
Managing Editor
Jessica Diamond

Senior Designer
Eriko Shimazaki
Designer
Lara Collins

Photography Editor
Sophie Corben
Photography Assistant
Robin Key

Sub Editors
Sarah Frank
Stephen Patience
Alison Willmott
Editorial Assistant
Ella Marshall
Interns
Jane Duru
Luke Sprague

**Wallpaper* Group
Editor-in-Chief**
Tony Chambers
Publishing Director
Gord Ray

Contributors
Sara Henrichs
Jasmine Labeau
Meirion Pritchard
James Reid
Ellie Stathaki

Wallpaper* ® is a
registered trademark
of IPC Media Limited

First published 2006
Second edition (revised
and updated) 2008
Third edition (revised
and updated) 2009
Fourth edition (revised
and updated) 2011
© 2006, 2008, 2009
and 2011
IPC Media Limited

ISBN 978 0 7148 6204 0

PHAIDON

Phaidon Press Limited
Regent's Wharf
All Saints Street
London N1 9PA

Phaidon Press Inc
180 Varick Street
New York, NY 10014

Phaidon® is a registered
trademark of Phaidon
Press Limited

www.phaidon.com

PHOTOGRAPHERS

Christopher Griffith
Oriental Pearl TV Tower,
pp010-011

Xiaoyang Liu/Corbis
Shanghai city view,
inside front cover

Tony Law
Café Sambal, p041

Simon Menges
Rockbund Art Museum,
pp036-037

**Mori Building
Company Limited**
SWFC, p013

Frank Palmer
MOCA, p034

Peartree Digital
Banmoo incense
holder, p083
Feiyue shoes, p085

Andrew Rowat
People's Park, pp014-015
Urbn, pp024-025
Quingpu, pp068-069

Jan Siefke
Shanghai Art
Museum, p012
Shanghai Sculpture Space,
pp070-071
Cha Gang, p078

**Jan Siefke/
Bartosz Kolonko**
Waterhouse, p017
Ritz Carlton, p027
JIA, p028, p029
Downstairs with
David Laris, p033
Noodle Bull, p035
Lune, pp046-047
Maison Pourcel,
pp048-049
Xibo, pp052-053
The Apartment, p058
Jiang Qiong Er, p063
Chinese Pavilion,
pp066-067
Shang Xia, pp074-075
The Villa, pp080-081
Aegis Shanghai,
pp086-087
The Peninsula Spa,
pp090-091
Espa, Ritz Carlton, p092
Evian Spa, pp094-095

Siefke/Huang
Zhujiajiao, pp098-099,
Fuchun Resort, pp100-101,
pp102-103

Charlie Xia
Drop, p039

Huang Yunhe
Yè Shanghai, p044

Judy Zhou/Fototeca
Park Hyatt, p022, p023
Lan Club, p038
M1NT, pp042-043
Kee Club, p050, p051
100 Century Avenue,
pp060-061
Spin Ceramics, p076

SHANGHAI
A COLOUR-CODED GUIDE TO THE HOT 'HOODS

JINGAN
The financial district is a white-collar world of high-rises and workers letting off steam

XINTIANDI
This Disney-does-dining pleasure quarter proves that heritage isn't what it used to be

THE BUND
The epicentre of the city's Western past now looks to Western retail for its future

FRENCH CONCESSION
Find the city's best old architecture here: a mix of art deco delights and Communist chic

PUDONG
This area is a lesson in how you turn farmland into a virtual Dubai in just two decades

PEOPLE'S PARK
The cultural hub of a commercial city, this is a good place to ease yourself into Shanghai

For a full description of each neighbourhood, see the Introduction.
Featured venues are colour-coded, according to the district in which they are located.